AFFIRMING

Dominic Walker OGS

THE
MINISTRY OF
DELIVERANCE

Series Editor: Jeffrey John

DARTON · LONGMAN + TODD

First published in 1997 by
Darton, Longman and Todd Ltd
1 Spencer Court
140–142 Wandsworth High Street
London SW18 4JJ

in association with

Affirming Catholicism
St Giles Church
No 4, The Postern
Wood Street, The Barbican
London EC2Y 8BJ

ISBN 0–232–52222–7

The views expressed in this booklet are those of the
author and do not necessarily reflect any policy
of Affirming Catholicism

Designed by Bet Ayer
Phototypeset by Intype London Ltd
Printed and bound in Great Britain by
Page Bros, Norwich

Affirming Catholicism

Affirming Catholicism is a movement (not an ecclesiastical party) which exists to do two things. We affirm our confidence in our Anglican heritage; and we seek to renew and promote the Catholic tradition within it. Our aim is to explore, explain and share with others both inside and outside the Church a lively, intelligent and inclusive Catholic faith. In the words of our Trust Deed:

> It is the conviction of many that a respect for scholarship and free enquiry has been characteristic of the Church of England and of the Churches of the wider Anglican Communion from earliest times, and is fully consistent with the status of those Churches as part of the Holy Catholic Church. It is desired to establish a charitable educational foundation which will be true both to those characteristics and to the Catholic tradition within Anglicanism . . . The object of the foundation shall be the advancement of education in the doctrines and the historical development of the Church of England and the Churches of the wider Anglican Communion, as held by those standing within the Catholic tradition.

Our Publications

These are offered as one means of presenting Anglican Catholic teaching and practice in as clear and accessible a form as possible. Some cover traditional doctrinal and liturgical themes; others attempt to present a well-argued Catholic viewpoint on issues of debate currently facing the Church. There is a list of our series of booklets on page v.

The present series of booklets is provided, where appropriate, with summaries to sections, and suggested questions which we hope will facilitate personal study or discussion in groups. Other titles in the series are:

To order these publications individually or on subscription, or for further information about the aims and activities of Affirming Catholicism, write to:

The Secretary
Affirming Catholicism
St Giles Church
No 4, The Postern
Wood St
Barbican
London EC2Y 8BJ

Tel 0171 638 1980
Fax 0171 638 1997

Booklets in the Affirming Catholicism series

About the Author

Dominic Walker is co-chairman of the Christian Deliverance Study Group, a group of priests and psychiatrists responsible for training Bishops' Advisers in deliverance ministry.

A priest of the Oratory of the Good Shepherd, educated at Kings and Heythrop Colleges in London, he is a contributor to the book *Deliverance* and is currently Vicar of Brighton.

Contents

Introduction

My doorbell rang at midnight. A young couple stood there looking terrified and hardly able to speak. 'We have a ghost', they said. 'Please come and help – please get rid of it.' I went back with them to their flat and they pointed to the corner of the bedroom where they had 'seen' a large black animal looking menacingly at them. 'We're not on drugs and we haven't been drinking', they tried to reassure me and yet they were plainly scared out of their wits. Was this just vivid imagination? Did they have a ghost? Did they need counselling or did the flat need exorcising? This was my first encounter with the ministry of exorcism, or deliverance as it is now called.

A number of such incidents with people claiming to have ghosts, poltergeists or hauntings or people claiming to be possessed by evil spirits or harmed by occult involvement led to the Bishop of Exeter setting up a commission comprising Roman Catholic and Anglican members, theologians and psychiatrists who, in 1972, issued their report entitled *Exorcism*. Its main recommendation was that:

It is much to be desired that every diocesan bishop should

appoint a priest as diocesan exorcist, and that in each province centres of training should be established.[1]*

The tragic Barnsley case, in which after an attempted exorcism a man murdered his wife, led to the House of Bishops issuing guidelines in which they said that the ministry of exorcism must be:

carried out (a) in collaboration with the resources of medicine, (b) in the context of prayer and sacrament, (c) with the minimum of publicity, (d) by experienced persons authorised by the diocesan bishop and (e) followed up by continuing pastoral care.[2]

Today, each diocesan bishop has someone to look after this area of ministry and in many dioceses there is a small team of people sometimes comprising not only priests but also laity, psychologists and psychiatrists. The Christian Deliverance Study Group, whose members are priests or psychiatrists, arrange training conferences for those nominated by their bishops with a view to being authorised for this ministry.

Nowadays the term 'deliverance ministry' is often used in preference to the word 'exorcism', for whilst exorcism is a perfectly good New Testament word, it implies a rite to deliver someone from demonic possession. Such a rite is rarely appropriate even though a person may feel under some evil influence. The term 'deliverance ministry' is much wider and includes counselling, confession, anointing and Holy Communion as means of ministering to those who seek freedom from evil, whether the source of that evil is from within themselves or from some external influence.

*For references, see p. 56.

Jesus was an Exorcist

When Jesus sent out his disciples, the authority he conferred on them included the power which he himself demonstrated to cast out demons or 'unclean spirits':

> He called to him his twelve disciples and gave them authority over unclean spirits, to cast them out, and to heal every disease and every infirmity.
>
> (*Matthew 10:1 cp Mark 3:15, Luke 9:1*)

Many of the New Testament miracles are exorcisms, and there can be no doubt that Jesus was an exorcist. It is now sometimes argued that the Church needs to take literally what Jesus said or we shall be reprimanded for our unbelief. After all, the Church neglected the ministry of healing, and yet today we see it restored and bringing renewal to the life of the Church. Is not the same also true for the ministry of deliverance? It is an appealing argument; but it is too simplistic because in order to relate the New Testament world to the world today, we first need to look at how the New Testament world relates to the Old Testament world.

The background to Jesus' ministry in Judaism was a world considered to be full of demons who were fallen angels and servants of a fallen archangel known as Lucifer, Son of the Morning, the Light-bearer. (The name Lucifer first appears in Scripture in the Book of Isaiah as a title of the King of Babylon.) Elsewhere devils are 'hairy ones', and the chief of devils appears as a 'spoiler', the 'serpent' or a 'dragon'. As belief in many gods and devils gave way to a belief in the one God named Yahweh, so Satan (meaning 'adversary') originally appeared under the command of God as a kind of neutral prosecution counsel in Yahweh's heavenly court. He is seen most clearly in this role in the Book of Job where he is given the task of putting Job to the test. In Zechariah, Satan assumes more power and is fiercely rebuked by Yahweh. In the inter-testamental period, however, partly under the influence of neighbouring religions, Satan suffered a further decline and becomes a figure explicitly opposed to God. In this period the tradition arose that Satan had been ejected from heaven for pride and rebellion, and had come down to continue his rebellion on earth.

So, whereas in the Old Testament Satan is still subject to God, in the New Testament he is clearly seen as being in opposition to God, together with his own angels. Indeed, in the New Testament he is the archetypal enemy who tempts Jesus, enters people (and pigs) and is seen as being in direct opposition to God and the establishment of Christ's kingdom. Nevertheless, the Bible never presents a complete dualism with Satan as another god. He is pictured in the Old Testament as being under the control of God, and in the New Testament, though he has his own temporary domain as 'prince of this world', he is rebuked and ejected by

Jesus as a created being in need of control, and forced to retreat as Jesus' kingdom grows.

Michael Wilson, priest and doctor, writing on how we are to relate Jesus' ministry to the Church's ministry today, wrote,

> I personally feel under no pressure to believe in possession by evil spirits just because Jesus believed in them. I feel under no obligation to exorcise anyone simply because Jesus and his contemporaries did so. The reason I feel free in this regard is because I believe in the incarnation. Jesus was born a Jew in Bethlehem when Cyrenius was governor in Syria. He really was made flesh and partook of the family, social and religious life of his day. A great deal of disturbed behaviour was then perceived as if caused by possession. It was the usual way to perceive it in those days, in that culture. I have little doubt that Jesus also believed that the world was flat. That too, was the usual belief of his day. That is what for me it means that Jesus was true man – God accepting the limitations of first-century Jewish flesh and knowledge. This raises for the pastor the important question as to how he or she uses the Bible. How far are Jesus' attitudes to things like illness, evil spirits, race and marriage, a sociologically determined part of his Jewish culture? How far are his teachings divine insights? How do we discover truth in the culturally-created language in which truth must be expressed?[3]

We might also ask to what extent Jesus *used* rather than *believed* the ideas of his age. In pastoral situations we often have to meet people where they are, which is not to collude with them but rather to be in empathy with them. Jesus may well have done the same.

Jesus came to establish his kingdom, and the Synoptic Gospels portray the coming of Christ and the preaching of the kingdom as being a spiritual battle against Satan. All three Synoptic Gospels record the temptations of Jesus in the wilderness at the start of his ministry and the continual battle with the devil which then ensues. This culminates in the Passion when Satan enters Judas who then betrays his master (Luke 22:3; John 13:27).

Whatever the precise nature of Jesus' beliefs, there can be no doubt from the Gospel records that he was engaged in a fight against evil. In the Synoptic Gospels the emphasis is on the activity of a personal devil and his angels. There is a spiritual battle between Jesus establishing his kingdom with signs and wonders, giving sight to the blind, making the lame walk, cleansing lepers, giving hearing to the deaf, raising the dead and preaching good news to the poor (Matthew 11:4–6) and Satan, who is out to get Simon and the other disciples (Luke 22:31) and being responsible for possessing people (Mark 8:5, 9:20). Indeed, Professor Morna Hooker notes that in Mark's Gospel not only direct exorcisms, but also healing and even nature miracles, are seen as Jesus overcoming the works of the devil, because the devil is responsible for all illness and disharmony in nature. In *The Message of Mark* she writes,

> There is in fact no hard-and-fast line between the exorcisms and the miracles of restoration. The leprosy which made the man unclean, the fever that attacked Peter's mother-in-law, are regarded as personal forces which must

be expelled, like the unclean spirits, if the victim is to be cured. And since these forces are hostile to God, the establishment of God's kingdom involves their overthrow ... The same principle is to be seen in the nature miracles – in particular, in the stories of the stilling of the storm in chapter 4, and the walking on the water in chapter 6. The former of these takes the form of an exorcism narrative, with Jesus addressing the wind and the sea with words that he uses elsewhere in speaking to demons, and we need to remember that Mark would probably have attributed the storm to demonic powers.[4]

Other New Testament writings suggest a rather different way of seeing things. In the Synoptic Gospels the emphasis is on the activity of a personal devil and his angels, whereas in the Johannine writings, the Gospel and Epistles, there is less emphasis on personalised evil; one way in which John portrays the fight with evil is as a conflict between light and darkness.

In the Synoptic Gospels it is the devil who opposes the establishing of the kingdom of God, whereas in Paul's writings, notably in his letter to the Romans, it is human sin which hinders God's will. Paul writes that if we are slaves of sin it will lead to death, but if we are slaves of obedience it will lead to eternal life (Romans 6:16).

So it is perhaps not surprising that neither John's nor Paul's writings refer to exorcism. It would seem that the attitude to exorcism in the early Church depended much on the influence of the local leader. Dr Graham Twelftree, in his study of exorcism in the New Testament, entitled *Christ Triumphant*,[5] concludes that the different strands in the New Testament writings bear witness to different emphases in different first-century congregations and that the Johannine ones probably had less to do with exorcism than others.

In the Acts of the Apostles we find reference to exorcisms in the name of Jesus, and the early Fathers frequently taught their people to take exorcism seriously. In his book *Deliverance* Michael Perry concludes:

> Exorcism was common in the world of Our Lord's day, and Jesus was himself an exorcist. He seems to have discriminated between cases in which exorcism was appropriate and those where it was not. Exorcism was certainly practised by the earliest Christians, though probably it was more highly valued in some congregations than in others.[6]

That Jesus was able to distinguish between cases which needed exorcism and those which needed healing points towards the need for such discernment in the Church today.

Throughout the history of the Church, exorcism has been practised to a greater or lesser extent. Today, both within the Church in the West and in the secular world, there is a new interest in exorcism which has excited both Christian charismatics and Hollywood film producers. Indeed, there is a danger that it is being given a prominence in the ministry of the Church which is both unbiblical and pastorally worrying.

The first danger is a tendency to 'demonise' what is not demonic, and whilst it is true that the Bible refers to a spirit of jealousy, a spirit of bondage and a spirit of fear, it also refers to a spirit of grace, a spirit of truth and a spirit of glory. Whilst the former may be attributes of the demonic and the latter attributes of the Holy Spirit, there can be no biblical justification for seeing the former as states of demonic possession in need of exorcism. As Cardinal Suenens wrote in *Renewal and the Powers of Darkness,*

> No demon of lust was expelled from the adulterous woman (John 8), or from the woman of ill-repute mentioned by Luke (Ch. 7), or from the incestuous people of Corinth (1 Cor. 5). No demon of avarice was expelled from Zacchaeus, no demon of incredulity from Peter after his triple betrayal. No demon of rivalry was expelled from the Corinthians whom Paul had to call to order.[7]

Secondly, when exorcism is carried out in an over-zealous way, it often only ministers to the spiritual nature of the person and ignores their psychological and physical needs. It can encourage them to deny responsibility for their own conduct, and if unsuccessful, leave them with the feeling that they are evil and that God can't or doesn't want to help them. Thirdly, by concentrating on personal possession it is possible to neglect the need to fight evil to bring about peace and justice as signs of God's kingdom. In his doctoral thesis *Living in Two Worlds* Robert Solomon examines the ministry of Anglican and Protestant pastors in churches in Singapore where exorcism is a prominent part of their ministries. He recognises the weakness of scientists and theologians who want to over-humanise evil, but concludes that exorcism is rarely the proper response to evil, and that evil needs to be exposed and resisted with repentance, acceptance and integration. He gives a warning:

> Exorcism may distract the pastor from dealing with real expressions of evil, in personal and in corporate realms. It is here that we note a significant absence of social and moral discourse in the accounts of the pastors. Spiritual blindness to evil in self and society is the result of such a narrow view of evil.[8]

Perhaps today, as in the early Church, a congregation's attitude towards exorcism will depend largely upon the teaching they have received from their local pastor. Some will give it an important place in their ministries as a tool for the furtherance of God's kingdom, whilst others will see evil in a personal and sociological context with its remedy in repentance and political change. For some the devil will be personal, whilst for others it will be a term used to personify evil. Either way, it is important to take evil seriously and to be pastorally equipped for whatever ways in which evil may manifest itself.

Responding to Problems

People who feel they have a spiritual problem will want to find a spiritual solution. If they think the Church can't help, they may look for spiritual help elsewhere, turning perhaps to spiritualist mediums or occultists. The Church must always respond with the assurance that help is available, either because we have the resources ourselves, or because we know where to refer people for further help.

Most of us, of course, have learned how to present symptoms. If we go to see the doctor we know we shall be asked questions about our medical history, our bowels, our appetite and sleep. Similarly, when people feel they have a spiritual problem they present what they believe to be spiritual symptoms – cold spots, weird shapes and noises. Many will have watched films or videos about the paranormal and believe that there are malevolent forces which can attack them for no apparent reason, and many will have talked with friends or neighbours who will have shared their own paranormal experiences.

It is therefore important for the pastor to take notes as the tale is recounted. It will help to distinguish between the phenomenon the troubled person claims to have witnessed and the interpretation they have given to it. It will also help to put it in some kind of chronological order (for few people begin at the beginning), and by looking at the notes later, it is possible to see if the story has improved with the telling! Notes also refresh the pastor's memory.

Most people will claim that they have a problem with either a place or a person. They will say they have a ghost, a poltergeist or some other kind of haunting, or they will say they have been cursed, possessed or have had some kind of bad experience from being involved in the occult or some New Age activity. It is important to let them tell the tale and to know that someone is listening and taking them seriously. Then the listener must put it all in context and ask whether they have had any other kind of experience like it, whether they have a psychiatric history; whether they are taking any medication or mood changing substances. Details of home and family life can be important, as can their religious and cultural background. It is, for example, not uncommon for Muslims living in a Christian country to seek help from Christians because they believe that any evil spirits must be Christian spirits needing Christian exorcism.

Some people are resistant to answering personal questions about their lives, perhaps because it is too painful or because they simply want some Christian 'magic' to happen so that they can return to their old ways. They reject any advice they don't want to hear or any other explanation for what is happening apart from their own. They usually have an understanding that people can be neatly categorised into body, mind and spirit, with the doctor, counsellor and priest treating the relevant parts. Deliverance ministry, however, requires an holistic approach.

The story of the woman with the haemorrhage is an example of holistic healing (Mark 5:25–34). It concerns a woman with perpetual menstruation which made her permanently unclean in Jewish society. Jesus didn't just let her touch him and be healed, and then disappear into the crowd. He asked who had touched him, and the poor, timid woman was brought from out of the crowd, accepted by Jesus with the loving words 'my daughter', and then restored to the community having been healed. It is a lesson that healing must take place within the community. This is particularly true when people seek deliverance ministry because so often there is an element of alienation involved, from themselves, their family or society.

Telling the same story, Luke, reputedly a doctor, omits the wonderful phrase 'she tried all manner of physicians and grew no better but rather grew worse' (Mark 5:26). This highlights a professional conflict which can arise when dealing with cases where the physical, spiritual and psychological are inter-related, for whilst acknowledging an holistic approach and working in co-operation with those from other professional disciplines, it is important to know our own professional boundaries. Jesus was able to heal and forgive sins at the same time, as in the case of the paralysed man (Mark 2:1–12) because he adopted an holistic approach. There is always the temptation for busy priests and doctors to want to deal with people quickly and to use sacraments or drugs to 'solve' the immediate problem rather than taking time to listen and discover the root cause of the problem.

Carl Jung and other psychologists have provided valuable insights into the human condition. They talk of the 'shadow' or dark side into which we suppress or repress painful material, much of which may have been stored from childhood. The point about the shadow is that it begins at our feet and we can't get away from it. For many people, sooner or later, there comes a time when there is a crisis in their lives and painful memories are stirred up. They have to face the darkness in their own *psyche* (soul) and this will need careful counselling whether by a pastor or psychotherapist. Images may emerge from the unconscious mind which are associated with the demonic and which need to be 'owned' and exorcised, although a gentle 'letting go' and surrender to the love of God will normally be more appropriate than a rite of exorcism.

Sometimes people will complain of dreams in which they see frightening images which they interpret as a demonic attack. Perhaps we undervalue the power and importance of dreams. Freud said that dreams are the royal road to the unconscious, and so by asking people about their dreams we are often enabled to see more clearly their anxieties and fears. Of course, many people will admit to dreaming but say that they can't remember their dreams. It is possible, however, to learn to remember dreams, but it requires a notepad by the side of the bed with a few minutes spent on waking up to try and recall them. From such recollections, it is often possible to discern the real cause of what are perceived as demonic attacks.

In the Bible, dreams are often seen as divine disclosures or warnings. Joseph in the Old Testament had prophetic dreams, the Magi are warned not to return to Herod, and the promise of Pentecost, fulfilling the prophecy of Joel, is that 'your young men shall see visions and your old men shall dream dreams' (Acts 2:17). Perhaps we might have expected it to be the other way round, with saintly old men given the visions and the young men as the dreamers; but no, dreams are God's gift to the wise who might have the wisdom and the experience to interpret them. That is not to say that we must expect divine revelations or world-changing disclosures from our dreams, but we can expect to discern from our dreams those areas of our lives which need attention – perhaps an area of unforgiveness, some hidden pain or hurt, something we have put off doing, something that needs to be taken to God in prayer. A dream may be God's gift to help us to discern and banish the demons which are within ourselves.

It is important to get the whole picture when ministering to someone who feels afflicted by evil and to provide both reassurance and firmness. It doesn't help to collude with their theories, but it does help to provide support and comfort, and the knowledge that they are in safe and good hands when they feel under demonic attack or evil influence. Pastors also need advice and assurance in dealing with areas of ministry with which they may be unfamiliar. The diocesan advisers mentioned in the introduction are willing to provide such support and supervision.

I once witnessed a young British Rail guard handle

a drunken vagrant who had boarded a train without a ticket. The guard was firm and told the aggressive passenger that he could not travel without a ticket, but he also constantly assured him that he would not be put off the train in the middle of nowhere. We often need to provide that kind of support, fixing the boundaries with firmness and not giving in to pleas for exorcism on demand, but at the same time providing comfort and assurance that we are willing to help and will not abandon those seeking help in the middle of nowhere.

Poltergeist Activity

The most common paranormal problem is the poltergeist. The poltergeist, as its name suggests (*poltern* is German for 'crashing around'), has often been understood to be the noisy ghost or the mischievous spirit which enters a home and causes havoc by flinging objects around the room and interfering with the electricity. In some cases, families have been so disturbed by this invasion of their home that, in panic, they have moved to get away from it, only to find that the poltergeist moves into their new home days after they do. It is not surprising that families experiencing such events should think that some unwanted spirit has invaded their home. Their cry for help is for someone to come and exorcise their home so that they can be left in peace.

However, it is now commonly accepted by those involved in the ministry of deliverance that poltergeist activity is not caused by an external power but by a member of the household under stress. Studies in parapsychology, both in the United States and this side of the Atlantic, give credence to the explanation that poltergeist activity is caused by psychokinetic energy emanating from a member of the household under great stress. J. Scott Rogo, in his study entitled *The Poltergeist Experience*,[9] echoes the experience of many involved in deliverance ministry which is that about two-thirds of the cases involve adolescents, and that the root cause seems to be a denial of feelings.

A young person going through puberty usually has few close friends with whom to talk about personal problems and anxieties, and is unable to communicate with his or her parents. I can give two examples to illustrate this.

A family of 'born again' Christians was experiencing poltergeist activity. They had curtains billowing at a window where there was no detectable draught. Electric lights began to flicker, an electric clock started to go backwards and then religious objects would be found thrown on the floor. On one occasion the Bible was thrown across the room whilst they were having a family prayer session. Thinking they had a demonic attack, they prayed for deliverance and then began a fast, but by the end of the fast things were worse rather than better, so they decided to call in the elders of their particular church who confirmed that it was indeed demonic possession. The elders anointed the doorposts and windows of the house and commanded the demons to leave. Again, the activity increased and the family were banned from attending their church on the grounds that they had invited demons into their house and were hiding something from God and needed to repent. The family in desperation called in the local vicar.

At the centre of the activity was their 11-year-old son. When away from his parents he told the vicar that he didn't like his parents' church and was play-acting and pretending to share their faith but he hated having to go to church twice on Sundays and join in the family prayer sessions. The vicar recognised that the boy was receiving mixed signals from his parents. They told him how precious he was and how much they loved him, but then added that they loved him so much that they only wanted him to be saved and to know the Lord. The boy did not recognise this as unconditional love, and felt that he had to pretend to share his parents' faith to gain their love. The vicar counselled the family together and assured them that they were not under demonic attack and within days the activity died down.

Another case involved an Asian family living in England. Poltergeist activity occurred in the family home and to a lesser degree in the family-run corner shop. They said they had a 'jinni', but sent for a Christian priest rather than a Muslim leader on the assumption that it must be a Christian jinni. The vicar visited the home and was only allowed to speak with the men of the house with the excuse that one daughter was too busy studying for her GCSEs and his wife and other daughter were working in the shop. He asked his curate to call on the women of the household separately. She soon realised that there was a problem with the 16-year-old daughter who was studying for her exams and arranged to see her alone after school. The girl was living a double life – a Western one at school and a Punjabi one at home. Her father told her that after her exams she would be sent to Pakistan where he had arranged a marriage for her. The girl admitted that the poltergeist activity began soon after. After counselling, she was informed of her legal rights, then the help of the local Imam was sought and when the girl's father was persuaded to cancel the wedding, the poltergeist activity ceased.

Poltergeist activity involving adolescents often arises where there is a conflict between the young people and their parents involving a moral, religious or cultural difference. In cases where an adult is the agent of the activity this is often the result of a denial of feelings. Cases have been known where adults have been denying marital breakdown, homosexuality, adultery, HIV, bereavement or cancer.

When poltergeist activity is present it is not a case for exorcism. Indeed it is likely to make matters worse because the person under stress or in denial, when receiving the wrong kind of help, may through their stress increase the psychokinetic energy exacerbating the paranormal activity still further. So the person creating the psychokinetic energy needs to be persuaded to 'own' his or her poltergeist and to accept responsibility for it. Some will greet with great relief the knowledge that they don't have a malevolent spirit. Others will have such strong feelings of denial that they will not be prepared to accept this explanation, or indeed that they have any inner turmoil, and will therefore still want an exorcism. Whilst they may be offered appropriate prayers and a blessing, experience shows that they must be given time to absorb the explanation. Many come back later, having accepted it and prepared to admit some inner conflict.

This is illustrated by the case of a family where quite violent poltergeist activity was taking place. On occasions, the family returned to their home to find it upside down as if they had been burgled, and yet, with no sign of a forced entry or anything missing. The father of the family also described how a crucifix he was wearing had bent and could not be bent back into shape and also how he felt a force trying to take control of his steering when he drove his car. He said that he had recently had a conversion experience and his children had been baptised and he and his wife had been confirmed. He was sure that God had given him a new beginning and his wife said that he was a completely changed person. He was no longer violent and had given up drinking and gambling. He now cared for her and the children and his Christian faith meant everything to him. He had previously, however, lived a life of violent crime and had spent years in prison. His new-found faith and his past seemed to be in conflict and as much as he tried to deny the past it was still there and he couldn't put it behind him in the way that he expected. He was assured that he had been forgiven and he accepted this by denying his guilt. After much agonising he made a very tearful confession and the poltergeist activity stopped almost immediately.

This chapter would not be complete without a warning and a reflection. The warning is that sometimes people fake poltergeist activity either to get attention, media publicity or even in the hope of being re-housed. The members of the Christian Deliverance Study Group have invented the name 'phoneygeist' to describe this! Fraud or attention seeking is not uncommon.

And here is a reflection. If by denying their feelings

people can create an energy so powerful as to move objects, perhaps we should not be too surprised when wonderful things happen in response to prayer by people who are in touch with their feelings and united in their love of God.

Ghosts

Ghosts are described as coming in all shapes and sizes – tall and short, male and female, human and animal, solid, semi-solid and opaque. Sometimes only one person sees the ghost, but then tells others who also see it. Sometimes different people, at different times, without forewarning or foreknowledge see the same ghost, thus suggesting a degree of objectivity about the apparition. What can we make of all this, and is there more than one explanation for the appearance of ghosts?

People often think that a ghost must be an unrested soul, someone who has died but has not gone to their rest and has returned to haunt them, but this is rarely the explanation. Some ghosts require a paranormal explanation (see chapters 6 and 7), but most can be explained as being some form of psychological projection.

A number of people (it has been estimated as being as many as one in six) see the ghost of their loved one soon after suffering a major bereavement. Sometimes they find it comforting to feel that their loved ones are still around and making themselves known; sometimes they find it distressing and feel that their loved ones are not at rest and have returned to seek their help. This kind of experience is part of the process of coping with the early stages of bereavement when the feeling of loss is beginning to surface, and the 'holding on' feelings have not been able to give way to the 'letting go'. In the very early stages, usually before the funeral has taken place, people are often in a dazed state and will even call for a taxi to take them to the hospital, only to realise when it arrives that they did it automatically and it hasn't fully registered in their minds that their loved ones are no longer there. Sometimes, once the loss has begun to register, people will describe seeing their loved ones sitting in their usual chair or hearing them call for them, or they will smell their pipe or perfume. Sometimes they will see them walking towards them in the street, only to realise as they get closer that it is someone else. In most cases, the departed person appears in solid form wearing familiar clothing.

A man who had recently lost his wife described how he had seen her get into bed with him and that he cuddled her and then went to sleep. In the morning she was not there. He told his daughter of this experience and the following day she 'saw' her mother walking down the stairs of her house which was some distance away from her father's home. The father and daughter were obviously very close and they told me that the mother had been ill in hospital for a while but they hadn't expected her to die. The priest recognised from the name of the hospital ward that she was being treated for cancer but when he mentioned cancer, they reacted very strongly and the father said, 'I don't allow that word in this house.' At the burial there was an unfortunate incident – the hole in the ground was too small for the coffin and they had to wait for the grave-diggers to enlarge it. They interpreted this as mother not wanting to leave them. It seemed evident that they had not come to terms with her being terminally ill and both found it very hard to accept. They were convinced that mother's appearances were because she didn't want to leave them, but they also had to come to terms with the fact that she had. In bereavement counselling they came to acknowledge that the ghost of mother was their own projection brought about by their inability to accept her death.

Psychological projections appear to account for most sightings of ghosts. That is, someone under stress is projecting an image from the unconscious mind and 'seeing' it as an apparition. It is very real to them, but not to anyone else, although of course sometimes in an emotionally charged situation there can be an hysterical reaction and others start seeing it as well. It is important to avoid telling anyone that they are 'imagining' a ghost, because they think they are being accused of lying about something that is very real to them. In a strict sense they *are* imagining it, because they are creating an image from the unconscious mind; but it is perhaps best to explain it as being like a vivid dream. Though not real to anyone else, dreams are a very real experience to those who dream them, and may be a way in which they are being shown some deep fear or concern with which they need help.

Sarah was a woman in her late thirties, although she looked much older. At night she claimed she was attacked by a large creature which looked like a huge bat with a beak and talons. She said it came into her bedroom and attacked her in bed and she showed the marks it made on her neck. She also claimed that some evil force kept trying to push her down the stairs of her house where she lived alone. She had called in a couple of mediums to cleanse the house but without success. A Pentecostal minister had visited and said prayers of exorcism but the attacks at night had grown worse. A Catholic priest told her that spirits are spiritual and cannot do physical harm and that the marks on her neck must be self-inflicted. It seemed that this large frightening ghost represented some deep anxiety in her life and the physical attacks at night indicated some sexual or other physical fear. When this was suggested to her she began to cry and her story slowly emerged. Her husband was in prison for having sexually abused his daughters who were now in care. She, too, had served a short prison sentence for colluding with her husband. She had access to her daughters and had begun to re-build a relationship with them, but her husband was now due for parole and she feared that she would be refused access to them and that he would sexually abuse her. She needed to 'own' the ghost and to recognise the depth of the fear inside herself and make her own decisions about the future.

A ghost may, of course, be an hallucination brought about by lack of sleep, illness or the use of alcohol or drugs. Even so, the ghost is likely to be a projection from the unconscious mind, even if the simplest way to prevent a re-occurrence is to deal with the physical cause. But in those cases where the appearance of a ghost can best be explained as either a bereavement experience or a psychological projection, appropriate pastoral care is required. Some cases will require bereavement counselling; others will require gentle probing to discover the source of the projection and to encourage the person to acknowledge it as part of themselves and to seek help in dealing with it.

Place Memories

There are various places which are reputed to have ghosts. Usually it is claimed that they not only appear, but also walk around and sometimes carry out various actions. In some ways it appears like a video replay, in which the same action is repeated each time the apparition is seen. It could, the sceptics would say, be a matter of folklore and psychological suggestibility, so that the story is planted in someone's mind causing them to expect to see the apparition, then, after a few drinks, or in poor light, they see the ghost just as they had imagined it to be. Such an explanation may well account for some cases.

There are, however, cases where people have not been forewarned and where different people at different times and without collusion have witnessed the same ghostly happening. This indicates some degree of objectivity where a psychological explanation will not suffice. One theory which is now fairly well accepted by those involved in deliverance ministry, is that places absorb memories which can be 'replayed' at a later date. These are known as place (or trace) memories.

Many people will have experienced feeling either at peace or uncomfortable in certain places. Cathedrals, churches and holy shrines often seem to have absorbed the prayers of the centuries; and even a home can feel a happy place where people have lived in love, security and peace, so that this feeling is sensed not only by those who live there but by visitors as well. Conversely, there are places where people feel ill at ease; it has been reported that the birds don't sing over Auschwitz and that flowers don't grow at other sites of torture. It is perhaps not surprising that some Jews want the Carmelite nuns to be removed from their monastery at Auschwitz to a monastery outside the grounds, partly because they want it to be preserved as an evil place and as a reminder of the suffering of the Holocaust.

Place memories appear to be simply memories and neither good nor bad in themselves, although they are normally re-energised by a person or sometimes by a similar event taking place. A place memory would appear to be an event from the past being re-played in the present. The Greek word *anamnesis* translated in English as *remembrance* means to make effective in the present an event from the past. At the Eucharist, the Church makes present and effective again the mighty acts of God and so the Eucharist is much more than a memorial meal. It is interesting that such a word should be in the vocabulary of an ancient civilisation whilst there is no equivalent word in English.

Place memories appear to be attached to a particular place and re-energised either by trauma to the place or by trauma to a person in the place. One commonly recounted place memory concerns a fox hunt which was sometimes seen to pass through the room of a large house. People witnessed the fox, followed by the hounds and the huntsmen on horseback. When alterations were made to the room and the floor level was raised, the next time the hunt was witnessed, the witnesses didn't see the fox or the hounds but only the top half of the huntsmen on horseback.

Place memories also occurred when a middle-aged couple bought a large house in Yorkshire which was in need of a great deal of modernisation. Each time they carried out a major work, they would see a little old lady appear to open a door in a wall and walk through the house. She used to leave behind a smell of either cigars or oranges. After a number of appearances, also witnessed by unsuspecting guests, they carried out some research into the history of the house at a local library and found a picture of their little old lady who had lived in the house some two hundred years previously. When they made alterations to the wall through which she was seen to appear, they discovered that there had indeed been a door in that particular place. But since the renovation has been completed she has not been seen.

There are extraordinary stories of occasions where people who are experiencing stress or trauma appear to spark off the memory. A married couple who lived in the country were awakened in the middle of the night by the arrival of an ambulance and police car outside their house. They went downstairs to find a distressed woman who had been passing in her car and witnessed an accident in which she saw a car hit a motorcycle and a following car run over the motorcyclist. At the suggestion of her two passengers who had also witnessed the accident, she drove on to the nearest phone box to call the emergency services and then returned to the scene. On returning to the scene there was no sign of such an accident having taken place. The woman and her passengers described the accident in some detail and one of the ambulance crew said that he had been called to that exact spot some 10 years previously when such an accident had taken place. The couple in the house were quite distressed because they had that day returned from the funeral of their 19-year-old son who had been killed in a motor-cycle accident.

Place memories appear to be triggered by trauma and are observable by those who are present, and as with most events different witnesses will often recall the event with variations in detail. But as a memory in itself appears to be neutral, it is not a case for exorcism. It is, however, appropriate to discover what traumatic events or what particular stress may have sparked off the memory and for appropriate pastoral care to be given.

It is also possible for a place memory and poltergeist activity to take place at the same time; the person under stress and creating the energy which causes poltergeist activity may also be energising the place memory. In such cases witnesses may observe an apparition like a video replay as well as interference with electricity and the projection of objects.

A somewhat different kind of place memory can be present when a place feels evil or uncomfortable. This may simply be an emotional feeling sensed by a number of people, or it may be associated with such things as cold spots or the 'presence' of some evil force. Whilst this could be someone psychologically projecting personal problems on to a place, it may also be due to the place having been associated with something evil. There have been problems associated with places which have been used previously for Satanic activities, illegal abortions, child prostitution or even homes where there has been a succession of marital breakdowns. In such cases, the celebration of the Eucharist and a blessing will help to overcome evil with good and to restore a feeling of peace. The service for the blessing of a home usually contains some prayers of deliverance and it is advisable to use this, together with the celebration of the Eucharist, rather than simply a service for the exorcism of a place, for which there is no biblical warranty. There is a biblical warning about exorcising evil and not replacing it with good (Matthew 12:43–45). The presence of Christ in the Eucharist and the invocation of God's blessing are normally sufficient in such cases, although where, for example, a church has been deliberately desecrated and defiled, a service of re-consecration is appropriate.

The phenomenon of place memory points towards the significance of memory within religious tradition. At the Jewish Passover there is a solemn recalling of the mighty acts of God, accompanied by appropriate actions – the eating of *harosheth* and the bitter herbs, the lamb bone on the *seder* dish, the drinking of wine, and the eating of unleavened bread and the setting of a place for the prophet Elijah. All these actions recall the past, are celebrated in the present, and point to the future. The Eucharist, with its origins in the Passover celebration also recalls the past, celebrates Christ's presence and looks forward to the heavenly banquet. Good memories need ritual to keep them alive in a way in which painful memories do not.

In the ministry of healing, the healing of memories plays a not insignificant role, but whole communities retain a consciousness of wrongs done to them, of persecutions suffered and of wounds unhealed. Whenever they sense an injustice done to them, the memory is ignited and acted out. South Africa and Northern Ireland are two such examples of places where long-term repentance, forgiveness and trust will be needed to heal the memories of the past.

The Unrested Dead

In recent years there has been a renewed interest in the idea that the departed can make their presence known or felt this side of the Grave. The New Age movement teaches 'channelling' which is a variation of spiritualism in which the departed give guidance to the living. On the other hand, Dr Kenneth McAll, in his book *Healing the Family Tree*[10] expounds his theory that some of the departed are unrested and seek help from the living.

It is not uncommon for people to believe that all ghosts are the ghosts of those who have died and have returned to or never left this world. There are however other explanations for ghosts, and cases of the dead re-appearing are comparatively rare.

It is important not to confuse unrested souls with the apparition seen by someone going through a major bereavement experience, to which earlier reference has been made. In such cases the apparition is only seen by those in a state of unresolved grief, whereas in the case of unrested souls, as in the case of place memories, the apparition is seen by different people and at different times and without any collusion. The main difference between a place memory and an unrested soul is that in the case of the former the apparition appears to carry out an independent act, whereas in the case of the latter, the ghost does not normally move but seems to want to make contact with the people to whom it appears, who may well be total strangers.

In an article entitled *The Biblical Justification for Exorcism*, Henry Cooper states:

> The idea of unquiet souls, or disembodied spirits of human beings lingering to plague the living, is not Christian . . . Exorcism is dealing with evil, with demons, located in persons or places, not with human spirits – there is, indeed no evidence that human spirits can or do exist apart from either this-worldly or that-worldly bodies.[11]

Father Cooper appeared to be making two important points. Firstly, the dead do not come back to torment us, and secondly, they will have some kind of body and therefore not appear as disincarnate spirits. In the same article, he draws a parallel between the Resurrection appearances of Christ and our own life after death. He says that Resurrection implies that the person retains three qualities. The first is that the person can be recognised as being the same person that he or she was before death. Secondly, that the person can express himself or herself, and thirdly that he or she can act. In other words, the dead are not mere spirits but have a body as was demonstrated in Jesus' own resurrection appearances, and as the credal statement about the resurrection of the body implies.

It is difficult, therefore, to know the exact nature of an unrested spirit. The person is plainly dead but are they risen? They appear to meet some of the criteria mentioned above in that they can be recognised, but they do not express themselves fully or appear to be able to act, except in a very limited way. It is hard to know what to make of this and to know what it says about the nature of God. Perhaps we may guess that it is not God who refuses to give eternal life, but the dead person who refuses to accept it. Some of the circumstances surrounding experiences of the unquiet dead might suggest this.

Sometimes the dead person has had an exceptionally strong attachment to a place or a particular possession and appears to have returned to be near it, as if unable to let go. Equally of course there is the possibility that the bereaved are unable to let go, but this doesn't explain sightings by others who had no particular emotional attachment to the dead person. In other cases the dead person appears to have some unfinished business and returns to give some message of repentance, or an apology to the living, or to complete some project left uncompleted. In such cases, once the unfinished business has been completed, the apparition of the departed person is not seen again. Some of the Early Fathers explained such an occurrence as the work of an angel rather than the departed person. Occasionally the ghost is of a person who appears to have died unmourned, either because there were no relatives or friends, or even because they have not known of the death. We are now more aware of the problems that arise when the living are unable to mourn properly for the dead. Is it possible that the lack of mourning should somehow have an influence on the dead themselves?

Whenever the evidence points towards the presence of an unrested soul, the celebration of a Requiem Eucharist is customary. Those present should pray for the departed soul, and the saving acts of God should be solemnly recalled for the benefit of the unrested person that he or she may rest in peace.

Oppression and Possession

The Church has traditionally defined three levels of demonic influence. These are temptation, oppression and possession.

The Gospel accounts of Jesus' temptations indicate that temptation is designed to take us away from God. Everyone experiences temptation in their lives which they often resist, but to which they sometimes succumb, then need to seek forgiveness through repentance. However, for some people temptation may result in an obsession, as with someone who is burdened with the obsessive temptation to commit a sexual offence. In such cases counselling and possibly psychiatric help will be needed.

Oppression is the term used when a person appears to be under some evil influence, whether through involvement with evil or occult practices or through having been cursed or through what appears to be no fault of their own. A person may have been cursed or believe themselves to be cursed, and whilst much of the power of a curse is in the mind of the sufferer, studies in other cultures suggest that there is more to it than that. It is, of course, unwise to plant in someone's mind the suggestion that he or she has been cursed, but it is wise to pray for the lifting of a curse when it seems appropriate.

Oppression may result from deliberate sin, and here repentance, confession and absolution together with pastoral support and counselling are needed. It is, however, important to distinguish between those who have sinned and those who have been sinned against. For example, it is not uncommon to find people who are the survivors of abuse, particularly sexual abuse, who feel evil or unclean and who need specialist help.

Depression can be another reason why people believe themselves to be under demonic influence. Severe depression leads to a feeling of low self-esteem, guilt and despair which is sometimes accompanied by feelings of paranoia. The carer may also be persuaded to collude with the delusions in an attempt to find some explanation for such a distressing condition. Much depression is caused by suppressed anger, but in severe cases we must look to the psychiatrists for primary help.

Sometimes whole communities can appear to be afflicted by some evil oppression and sense that there is something which needs exorcising from their midst. The psychodynamics of any group are likely to be complex, with a great deal of projected material being thrown around, but identification of the evil in their midst can give communities the power to deal with it and bring about healing and renewal. This is perhaps best explained by a particular case.

A certain parish had faced one tragedy after another, and the congregation felt that they had more than their fair share of misfortune. The vicar had not faced such unhappiness in any parish before and his two pre-decessors were glad to have moved on. The local people didn't relate to the church; there was a great deal of gossiping in the pews, and church council meetings always ended in a row. As the vicar and churchwardens talked though the dynamics of the parish two particular people emerged as being at the root of much discontent. Both had deep resentments, one as the result of a bereavement and the other from rejection for ordination. It was, of course, important not to 'demonise' them and to project other people's feelings on to them, but it was possible to see how they were poisoning the parish. It was decided that their behaviour needed to be challenged and exposed, so that they could see it for themselves, and in the hope that their healing would bring healing to the whole community.

Possession may not be an everyday experience and yet we use 'possession language' in everyday speech. We may say, 'I don't know what possessed me' or 'It's as if the devil's got into him'. It describes something of the experience of a change in personality as if driven by some inner or external force. People may even believe that they have been taken over by a human spirit of someone alive or dead. We also use such language when we speak of being filled or possessed by the Holy Spirit, signifying some change in personality or behaviour brought about by an outside spiritual influence.

The Church speaks of 'demonic possession' whilst psychiatrists speak of 'possession syndrome' to describe the phenomenon of changed personality, where a person's will appears to be taken over, sometimes resulting in violent or unusual behaviour. There is a wide divergence of opinion among both theologians and psychiatrists as to the causation of such symptoms. The basic question for both is, by what can someone be possessed? Are they possessed by some demonic force from outside themselves, or are they possessed by something from deep within themselves, some aspect of their personality which appears to have lain hidden only to emerge and take over the person? Can a human being be possessed by the spirit of another person?

Possession or 'infestation' are the terms used when a demon or demons have taken over the whole personality and the sufferer is no longer able to control his or her own will. Possession states are very rare; oppression is much more common. A person claiming to be possessed may well be suffering from a psychotic illness. It is not unusual for psychiatrically ill people to have religious delusions and to believe that they have a special mission from God, or are under the influence of the devil, or that other people are demonic. In some cases the person may be a victim of other people's psychological projections. Being unable to cope with the evil or dark side of themselves these people may have projected it on to the sufferer. We always hate in others what we hate most in ourselves. This can happen within a family, and even charismatic church house groups and the monastic communities are not immune. The most vulnerable person in the group becomes the scapegoat, takes on the projected evil from the others, and believes himself or herself to be evil and in need of exorcism.

Schizophrenic sufferers often claim to hear voices from the devil or believe that they are being taken over by a demon. Sometimes they believe they are hearing voices from God. In 'Demon possession: Medical perspectives in a Western culture', Professor Andrew Simms, a psychiatrist, describes how priests and psychiatrists can work together within their own disciplines to help such people.

> The fact that a patient's religious or demonic experience has a psychological explanation does not prevent it from also having a non-psychological explanation. A person describes 'hearing God clearly telling me' to do this. The psychiatrist will want to examine the form of the experience and other associated psychiatric experiences – is this an auditory hallucination or not? A person looking at this from a Christian viewpoint will want to consider the person's other religious beliefs and also what is the result in action of this supposed message from God – 'by their fruit you will recognise them' (Matthew 7:16). These two approaches, far from being incompatible, are complementary.[12]

In a chapter on Possession Syndrome, the Christian Deliverance Study Group's book *Deliverance*[13] illustrates the frequent psychiatric conditions in which the sufferer may claim to be possessed, namely organic psychosis, hysterical neurosis, temporal lobe epilepsy and hysterical personality disorder.

In some cases people will claim to be influenced or possessed, for good or for evil, by dead people. There is the case of Rosemary Brown in south London who claimed to be influenced by the spirits of famous composers and to have composed their 'unfinished symphonies'. There is the case of Juan Jose Fong, a Chinese-Mexican who claimed to be possessed by the spirits of St Peter, St James, St Dominic and a doctor. Fong was observed in possession states speaking in different voices, a feature of so-called mystical possession as well as of so-called diabolical possession. This is a manifestation which Jung called 'autonomous complex'[14] in which each spirit functions like a separate personality subsystem. In his study of the Fong case, psychologist Marc Cramer concluded that the personal characteristics of the three 'saints' and the 'doctor' were compensations for inadequate aspects of Fong's own personality, and as such were part of a psychological struggle for integration.[15]

Three significant contributions have been made to the subject of exorcism by a philosopher, a psychiatrist and a psychologist. In 1921, T. K. Oesterreich, then Professor of Philosophy at Tübingen University, wrote a major work, *Possession and Exorcism*[16] in which he examined both mystical and demonic possession. In 1973, William Sargant, Professor of Psychiatry at St Thomas' Hospital, London examined possession, mysticism and faith healing in his study *The Mind Possessed*.[17] In 1980, Marc Cramer wrote *The Devil Within*.[18] Whilst approaching the subject from different religious and academic backgrounds their findings have much in common. They conclude that possession is a complex manifestation which involves very varied patterns of behaviour. The sufferer may be experiencing two or more emotional states at one and the same time which give the impression of an inner psychological conflict, or the sufferer may be experiencing a single compulsion, that of feeling possessed. Some states may be consciously induced and others occur more or less spontaneously.

Dr Oesterreich's study shows that possession and exorcism have been part of human experience in all cultures and in every age with common features, notably striking changes in voice appearance together with a changed personality. Dr Sargant also examines possession states in a number of cultures, religious and secular. He concludes that we have created both gods and demons in our own image, and that both belief and possession are physiological or psychological states capable of achieving good or evil. For Sargant, possession is a psychological, not a spiritual disorder. Marc Cranmer's study comes to three fundamental conclusions. Firstly, that the overwhelming majority of all reported cases of demonic possession are the result of hysteria or else are outright frauds. Secondly, that whilst manifestations of possession as something distinct from mythomania or madness may exist, this does not mean that 'possession' is actually caused by evil spirits or demons. Thirdly, there is every reason to believe that so-called demon infestation is a psychological, but not a supernatural event; the syndrome is not directly or exactly related to other mental disorders, but belongs to a separate category.

When we turn from these studies of a philosopher, a psychiatrist and a psychologist to that of a Christian theologian, we are presented with a different viewpoint.

Dr Graham Twelftree, in his book *Christ Triumphant*,[19] examines the background to New Testament thought, stating that at that time not everyone believed in demons and exorcisms, and that Jesus seemed to discriminate between those cases which needed exorcism and those which did not. He focuses on the symptoms which are traditionally associated with possession or possession syndrome, such as unusual strength, disregard for pain, disturbance when faced with Jesus, and voices which do not appear to belong to the sufferer. He challenges the view that Jesus' exorcisms fit any accepted modern diagnosis. Dr Twelftree is keen to point out that Jesus does not exorcise in an emotional way but by his own personal authority, as if his own goodness is directly confronting the forces of evil.

Theologians and scientists agree that there is such a thing as possession state, although they may differ among themselves as to its cause. Those with a belief in external demons will believe that the bizarre symptoms and change in character are brought about by some invasion from outside and that the sufferer can be cured by a rite of exorcism in which, traditionally, the demon or demons are bound and commanded to leave the person. Those who believe demons to be internal may see them as unintegrated parts of the sufferer's personality, parts which have been denied or suppressed and which under stress emerge to 'possess' and take over the sufferer, producing in the process extraordinary or paranormal phenomena. In both cases it can be argued from a Christian perspective that exorcism is an appropriate remedy, either because the power of Christ over demons is assured, or because the healing power of Christ is mysteriously at work releasing the psychological chains which have been imprisoning and overpowering the sufferer. In both cases the sufferer is released into 'the glorious liberty of the children of God' (Romans 8:21).

Possession states can be characterised by a change in tone and inflection of voice; speaking in different voices sometimes claiming to be different entities; convulsions; distortion of the face; paranormal manifestations; fear of and violent reaction to holy objects; blasphemy; violence and great strength; trance-like states; xenoglossolalia (the ability to speak and converse in a known foreign language). When the person appears to have been taken over they lose their will, or in psychological terms they lose control of their ego and superego functions. They appear to be taken over by forces outside themselves and utter or shout blasphemous and obscene remarks, or even imitate some symbol of evil, such as hissing and moving like a snake. When the possession state ceases, either spontaneously or as a result of exorcism, it is followed by exhaustion and amnesia.

It will be seen from the above description that a person in a possession state is in both a desperate and a vulnerable position. It is for this reason that the Church has clear rules governing the practice of exorcism. Traditionally, there are two types of exorcisms – the major exorcism and the minor exorcism. In a major exorcism, the exorcist addresses the demons in the name of Christ, binding them and commanding them to leave and not to return again. In a minor exorcism, which is used when oppression rather than possession is diagnosed, the prayer is addressed to God to free the person from evil. Such a petition is found in the Lord's Prayer and in the baptismal liturgy, in which the priest prays, 'May the Lord deliver you from the powers of darkness and bring you to the light and obedience of Christ'.

Conclusion

It has been said that Adam said to Eve, 'My dear, we live in a time of change'. Our world is constantly changing, although human nature remains much the same. The knowledge of evil and the need to deal with it have been with the human race from the outset. Every race, culture and religion has had an understanding of possession and exorcism, and of the need to be delivered from evil whether or not it is of our own making.

As we live in a time of change, the challenges facing the Church are also changing. Our society is intrigued by the paranormal as the number of films, videos and books on the subject indicates. Our society is also intrigued by the occult, and occult shops, magazines and courses are a growth industry. New Age philosophies and practices are advertised in most newspapers and magazines, and people today are bombarded with a range of alternative ideologies and belief systems. In contrast, the Church is presented in the media as being middle class, out of touch and obsessed with its own internal issues. Yet it is to the Church that people turn for help when the other paths turn out to be dead ends, or when the darkness inside or outside themselves overwhelms them.

The 'golden rules' in the ministry of deliverance are:

1. Always look for a natural or psychological explanation before going for the supernatural or paranormal one.
2. Bring love and reassurance. The *quality* of care often does more to help the situation than doing all the right things.
3. Do not collude with other people's prejudices or demonologies, but be sympathetic.
4. Always overcome evil with good and avoid any hint of Christian 'magic'.
5. Proclaim the victory of Christ in what is said and done; preach the gospel in each situation.
6. Seek help, advice and supervision.
7. Remember that deliverance ministry is only one area of ministry and don't give it a prominence it doesn't deserve.
8. Avoid too narrow a view of evil – and don't be blinded to the real evils in society and the battle for peace and justice.

Jesus, as we have seen, sent out his apostles with authority to heal the symptoms and causes of all humankind's sickness and sin – physical, psychological and spiritual. In all our struggles with evil, internal and external, we are fulfilling his commission, and we are promised the assurance of his presence and his victory. As we have seen, the ministry of deliverance calls for special gifts of discernment, wisdom and pastoral sensitivity; but it is equally clearly a ministry which is increasingly needed, and one which only the Church can supply.

Questions

Introduction

1. What does the word 'exorcism' suggest to you? Does 'deliverance' seem a better term, and if so, why?

2. Why do the Church authorities feel it is important to follow strict guidelines when handling the ministry of deliverance?

3. Do you have any personal experience of this ministry, or of related 'supernatural' phenomena?

Jesus was an Exorcist

1. Do you believe in a literal devil or demons? If not, how do you understand the passages in Scripture that refer to them?

2. How might some of the exorcisms decribed in the Gospels be understood today?

3. Why does the writer see the media's current interest in demons and exorcism as 'worrying'?

4. What are the personal and spiritual dangers of an excessive interest in supernatural evil?

Responding to Problems

1. What does the writer mean by saying that deliverance ministry requires a 'holistic approach'?

2. How many kinds of cases can you think of where physical, pychological and spiritual sickness might be hard to distinguish?

3. How may dreams be able to help us attain 'wholeness'?

4. How would you respond to someone who told you they felt oppressed by supernatural evil?

Poltergeist Activity

1. Do you have any personal knowledge, experience or evidence of poltergeist activity? Does it surprise you that it seems to be so well attested?

2. What do you understand by the term 'psychokinetic energy'? What difference does it make if a 'poltergeist' is explained as the manifestation of such energy, rather than as the effect of an outside power?

3. What do you think is the likeliest explanation of the fact that poltergeist activity tends to occur in households containing an adolescent?

4. What special care needs to be taken in dealing with activity of this sort?

Ghosts

1. Do you believe that ghosts exist objectively – i.e. outside the minds of those who see them? If you do,

who or what are they? If you don't, how do you explain the number of apparitions people claim to experience?

2. What do you understand by the term 'psychological projection'? What is the difference between 'psychological projection' and imagining or lying?

3. Imagine someone approached you claiming to be troubled by a ghost. What questions would you ask?

Place Memories
1. How likely does it seem to you that places or buildings can 'absorb' memories or particular events, or seem to generate an atmosphere of their own? Do you have any personal experience or evidence of this?

2. What role might auto-suggestion or group suggestion play in the development of 'place memories'? What about the cases where they seem to be ruled out?

3. Look up the word *anamnesis* in a theological dictionary. What is the difference between 'remembering' at the Eucharist, for example, and ordinary 'remembering'? Does this distinction help us understand the meaning of 'place memories' – or of 'remembering the departed'?

4. What does the phrase 'healing of memories' suggest to you? Do you think you have any unhealed memories? How do you recognize them? What can be done about them?

The Unrested Dead

1. What do you think happens when we die? Would the existence of 'unrested souls' fit in with your beliefs about death and the afterlife?

2. If such souls exist, what might be the reasons for their remaining in an 'unrested' state?

3. Why is the celebration of a Requiem Eucharist thought appropriate in the case of a supposed haunting by the departed? What are we doing when we celebrate a Requiem? What should be our prayer in such a situation?

4. What crucial difference is the writer drawing between apparitions of the departed to bereaved relatives and friends, and other apparitions to strangers and independent witnesses? How should this affect our pastoral approach?

Oppression and Possession

1. Distinguish between temptation, oppression and possession. Why is making the distinction important?

2. How might sacramental confession help with some cases of temptation and oppression?

3. What would you say if approached by someone who said that he or she was under a curse?

4. How would you recognise clinical depression? Why is it sometimes perceived by the sufferer as demonic oppression or possession?

5. How may communities sometimes seem to be

afflicted by 'supernatural' oppression? What other factors and interpersonal mechanisms may generate such a problem?

6. Do you think it is ever truly appropriate to speak of 'demonic possession' – that is, literal possession by an outside force or personality?

7. 'Psychosis' and 'schizophrenia' are technical words: what precisely do they mean? Why do they relate very closely to the phenomenon termed 'possession'?

8. One explanation of 'possession' is that it occurs when a severely repressed aspect of the personality breaks out and takes over. If this is so, how appropriate is a service of exorcism which purports to 'drive out' a supposedly external force?

9. Could a Christian speaking in tongues be said to be 'possessed'? How do you understand this phenomenon?

Conclusion
1. Consider the eight 'golden rules' which the author applies to the ministry of deliverance. What are the particular dangers which each seeks to avoid?

2. Who do you think should be allowed to exercise the ministry of deliverance in the Church, and under what circumstances? What special qualities do they need?

References

1. Ed. Dom Robert Petitpierre OSB, *Exorcism*, London, SPCK, 1972.

2. General Synod, *Report of Proceedings*, vol.6, no.2, July 1975.

3. Michael Wilson, 'Exorcism: A clinical/pastoral practice which raises serious questions', *The Expository Times* LXXXVI, 10 July 1975, pp.292–5.

4. Morna Hooker, *The Message of Mark*, Epworth Press, 1983, pp.42, 43.

5. Graham Twelftree, *Christ Triumphant*, London, Hodder and Stoughton, 1985.

6. Ed. Michael Perry, *Deliverance*, London, SPCK, 1987, p.109; revised 1995.

7. Cardinal Suenens, *Renewal and the Powers of Darkness*, London, Darton, Longman and Todd, 1983, p.17.

8. Robert Soloman, *Living in Two Worlds: Pastoral responses to possession in Singapore* Frankfurt, Peter Lange, 1994, p.288.

9. D. Scott Rogo, *The Poltergeist Experience*, Wellingborough, Aquarian Press, 1989.

10. Kenneth McAll, *Healing the Family Tree*.

11. Henry Cooper, *The Biblical Justification for Exorcism*, The Guild of St Raphael, pp.4, 5.

12. A. C. P. Simms, 'Demon possession: Medical perspectives in a Western culture', in Palmer, B., *Medicine and the Bible*, Exeter, Pater Nostra, 1986, p.188.

13. Ed. Michael Perry, op. cit.

14. C. G. Jung, 'The psychological foundation of the belief in spirits', first delivered as a lecture, July 1919.

15. Marc Cramer, 'Psychopathology and shamanism in rural Mexico: A case study of spirit possession', *British Journal of Medical Psychology*, 1980, pp.67–73.

16. Traugott K. Oesterreich, *Possession and Exorcism*, Causeway Books, New York, 1974 (originally published in 1921 as *Possession: Demoniacal & Other*).

17. William Sargant, *The Mind Possessed*, London, Heinemann, 1973.

18. Marc Cramer, *The Devil Within*, WH Allen, 1979.

19. Graham Twelftree, op. cit., p.199.

20. Michael Perry, *Gods Within, A critical guide to the New Age*, London, SPCK, 1992.